Teenage Girl's Survival Handbook

An A-Z guide to getting the Christian Life sorted

by
Eleanor Watkins

Kevin Mayhew

First published in 1998 by
KEVIN MAYHEW LTD
Rattlesden
Bury St Edmunds
Suffolk IP30 0SZ

0 1 2 3 4 5 6 7 8 9

ISBN 1 84003 228 6
Catalogue No. 1500214

Cover design by Simon Smith
Edited by David Gatward
Typesetting by Louise Selfe
Printed in Great Britain

Introduction

It's not easy being a teenage girl.

Those early teen years can be a mixture of excitement, anxiety, anticipation, frustration, fun, foreboding, discovery, achievement, mistakes, development, and so much more. You are changing and growing, physically, mentally and spiritually, at a rate of knots. Small wonder you sometimes feel totally freaked out!

Don't despair. All of us females went through basically the same things, and, yes, we still remember what it felt like. And most of us came out the other end relatively unscathed.

This A-Z was written in the hope that, in its pages, someone will find help, reassurance, guidance, an answer to their questions or encouragement to press on in their Christian life.

And, hopefully, maybe a couple of laughs along the way too. I'd be glad to know what you think.

ELEANOR WATKINS

*This book is dedicated to
all teenage girls everywhere,
and especially to my
daughter, Natasha, from
whom I have learned a
great deal over the past
few years.*

Acne

Acne is the pits and so are all the other types of spot, blemish, pimple and zit just waiting to erupt from your otherwise clear skin. Have you noticed how a spot won't show itself until the very day you have an important interview, or a special party, or there's a gorgeous new bloke at the youth club you'd really like to make an impression on? It's not a bit of use your mum or your best friend telling you the spot is miniscule and hardly visible without a magnifying glass, and that a bit of *Cover Plus* (*Zowee! It Zaps Zits!*) will completely disguise it. You *know* that it's huge, and red, and completely gross and off-putting.

Seriously, real acne is common among young people as it's hormone related.

Males suffer more than females, it's worse in people with oily skins, and usually clears up of its own accord by your early twenties.

If you're fourteen and spotty, that's not much consolation, but don't despair. Help is available. Severe acne can be controlled by medication from the doctor, but there are some things you can do to help yourself:

- Sunshine is beneficial (though be careful about sunburn).
- Wash the affected areas carefully twice a day with warm water and a mild, pure, non-perfumed soap (i.e. Simple soap).
- Tea Tree oil works wonders at clearing up spots.
- Antiseptic cream such as Germolene can help healing in spots that are infected.

Above all, don't pick or squeeze spots – this spreads infection and can leave scars.

Aids

Whatever your standpoint, AIDS is here and it's serious. AIDS is a killer with no cure as yet. Safe sex is repeatedly promoted as protection, but the only real protection is keeping sex within marriage. This may seem tough, but it's fact.

Nevertheless, there are myths about AIDS. The HIV virus is only passed on through the sharing of body fluids, as in sexual intercourse, contact with infected blood or using a dirty hypodermic needle. It is NOT passed on from lavatory seats, clothing, hugging, touching or even kissing.

AIDS is not the judgement of God, it is a tragic result of ignoring the rules God has laid down for our health and happiness.

Alcohol

It's not always recognised that alcohol is actually a powerful drug. Its effects are even stronger on a young person or a small person and girls are more susceptible than boys.

Alcohol is absorbed into the bloodstream more quickly on an empty stomach. It has a strong depressant action on the nervous system, slowing down the brain and affecting co-ordination, judgements and emotions. The short term effects of alcohol include headaches, nausea, vomiting, dehydration, accidents, aggression and hangovers. Inhibitions are lessened and judgement is impaired. Long term effects can be damage to the liver and heart, brain and nervous system, depression, personality changes and dependence.

An acceptable social habit? Work it out for yourself and have a read of Romans 6:13.

Animals

Animals are one of the comforts of life. A pet is always pleased to see you, usually welcomes a cuddle, listens to all your woes and doesn't answer back. The saddest thing about pets is that their life-span is short and sooner or later, they'll grow sick or old and die.

Losing a pet is a true bereavement, and takes time to get over. Cry for them as much as you need to, but don't feel guilty. Remember the good times you had together. When you're ready, welcome a new pet into your life and enjoy it.

Taking care of a pet is good discipline. It needs to be fed, exercised, groomed and kept clean, and you can't shove it into a garage or cupboard like a bike or a pair of roller-blades when you're tired of it.

A pet is for life!

Anorexia

See
Eating Disorders

Arguments

See
Quarrels, Families

Bible

Young Christians (and indeed all Christians) need regular portions of the Bible to nourish them, just as much as we all need three square meals a day to feed our bodies.

The Bible is a collection of books – history, poetry, teaching and story-telling – written by various authors under the inspiration of God. It tells of God's creation of the world, the history of its peoples, collected writings of its poets and prophets, all pointing to the coming of Jesus Christ, God's son, about whom the New Testament was written, and whose life and death is central to the Christian faith.

Bibles come in many translations and modern versions these days. The King James Authorised version has beautiful language and imagery, but some of the modern forms are easier to understand and relate to life in today's world. Some are paraphrased into modern everyday language, while others may even have cartoon-like illustrations. There are also Youth Bibles with specially marked passages of Scripture. Whichever you choose, a set of study notes is helpful to get you started and help you understand and apply what you are reading to your own life. It's an extremely valuable discipline to memorise Scripture verses, which are then stored away deep inside you for use when you need them. Bible study and discussion groups with other young people can be stimulating, exciting and a real source of discovery, encouragement and growth. (Read 2 Timothy 3:14 to 4:5.)

Bedrooms
See also **Privacy**

Your bedroom is the place where you go to relax, rest, sleep, enjoy privacy, read, study, listen to music, think, let your hair down and be yourself.

A bedroom is said to reflect the personality of its occupant. I hesitate to guess what yours says about you, because generally it is an eclectic mix of discarded clothing, wet towels, books, magazines, soft toys, sweet wrappers, bags, shoes and open drawers and cupboards! Posters of cuddly animals rub shoulders with gorgeous pop stars on the tastefully decorated walls, and the air is heavy with the scent of body spray. You have stuck drawing pins in places where pins ought not to be stuck, and a felt-tipped pen has leaked onto the cream carpet, where you flung it on failing to express your feelings in a letter to your last-but-one ex-boyfriend. At the same time, you knocked over a half-full coffee mug, which has left a brown stain that refuses to come out. Lush!

Whenever a friend is sleeping over, you have a blitz which leaves your room neat, dusted, vacuumed and free of clutter. The guest has to be careful of just one thing though; she must never, ever, open the cupboard door, or she is in danger of being buried alive in the avalanche of stuff that will burst out.

Boots
See also
Clothes, Fashion

In your mother's heyday, tight white shiny plastic boots were the essential footwear. That was the era of PVC macs, white lipstick and hairspray. Later came knee or thigh-high leather boots with platform-soles and stacked heels (they're back!) which elevated the wearer by six inches or so, made walking something of a hazard and were the cause of many a sprain, twisted ankle and pulled muscle. (Suede pixie-boots, ankle height and mostly flat-heeled, were much safer and more comfortable.)

Boots have come in all lengths, heel heights, fabrics, colours and styles, with cuffs, cut-outs, fringes, zips, laces and other forms of decoration. Your big black clumpy Doc Martens lasted for a long time, and have been replaced by tough Cats, wickedly expensive but so comfortable, sensible and trendy that your mother is thinking of saving up for a pair herself!

Best Friends

Everyone needs a best friend, though sometimes they can be a mixed blessing. A while ago your best friend was Louise, who proved traitorous by talking about you behind your back and then going off with your current boyfriend. Then there was Trudy, who had the habit of ignoring you when anyone more interesting came along (which seemed to be quite often).

At present your best friend is Samantha, with whom you get along pretty well, apart from the occasional difference of opinion. She does have a bit of an attitude problem, but you and she are quite happy to spend hours talking over the causes and effects of it. In fact, school hours are nowhere near long enough for this, and you find it necessary to spend several hours each evening on it as well. This adds up to quite a close relationship and also adds up to a rather large phone bill.

Ideally, a best friend should be loyal, supportive, discreet, generous, slow to take offence and quick to forgive. She should be willing to share, listen, advise, console, pick up pieces, and lend a shoulder to cry on and her new black velvet top for Saturday night. She should treasure her half of the *Friends are Forever* pendant you bought her and never, ever, ask for the other half back. She should never divulge a confidence or repeat a secret entrusted to her ears.

We live in a less than ideal world, and your best friend will probably let you down in at least some of these departments. Don't forget that it's possible that you will do the same.

Boredom

Life can be boring. At times it's very boring, like when there's nowhere to go, nothing to do and no one to do it with. It doesn't help when adults make remarks like 'If you're bored I can soon find something for you to do!' or 'I wish I had the time to be bored!'

Most adult conversations are boring as well. So are long car journeys with your parents. So are some books you have to read for your literature course. So are some church services. The list could continue.

Perhaps the best antidote to boredom is someone else your own age to be bored with . . . or maybe just considering someone else besides yourself . . .

12

Boys

Boys seem to appear on the scene when you are about eleven or twelve. They must have been there before, of course, but you probably only noticed them for their nuisance value.

Suddenly, they are everywhere, with long arms and legs and deeper voices, and a habit of looking at you out of the corner of their eye as you walk down the street.

Boys would like you to believe that they are tough, macho and independent. In fact, they have at least as many hang-ups and insecurities as girls.

It's cool to be on friendly terms with lots of boys, so don't be in too much of a hurry to meet that special one!

Boyfriends

See also
Relationships

It's a terrific morale-booster when a boy asks you out. You don't have to accept. Ask yourself some questions first:

- *Do you really like him?*
- *Do you trust him?*
- *What does he mean by 'Going out'*
- *What do YOU mean by 'Going out?'*

If you're a Christian you're wise to stick to boys who are Christians too. You may think you'll be able to influence that hunky non-Christian, get him converted and live happily ever after. It hardly ever works like that. More likely, you'll find yourself pulled in different directions which is uncomfortable if not downright painful.

If in doubt, take great care. Ask advice from your best friend, but also from trusted people a little older and more experienced. These could be a young couple at your church, or your youth leader, or even (horrors) your own parents. You'll be surprised how much they remember from their long-gone youth.

Don't fall into the trap of thinking any boy is better than no boy. On the other hand, you need to get to know as many as possible, so that you recognise a really good one when he comes along.

Bras

Bra sizes can create a lot of worry, but there's no need. Bust sizes vary a great deal and virtually all are normal. People develop at different rates, so don't be tempted to compare yourself with friends.

It's important though to get the right sized bra, one that fits comfortably and gives the right support. Wearing your older sister's cast-off is not a good idea, nor one that is grey and ancient and stretched out. Get fitted by a proper expert, and re-fitted as you grow.

Finally, never feel awkward about your developing bustline, whatever its size. Don't develop a round shouldered stoop to disguise it. Be proud that you're growing into an attractive woman.

Brothers

On the whole, brothers can be an advantage, especially older brothers. Older brothers are useful in many ways. They may even have trendy gear like shirts and jackets for the borrowing! (As long as they never find out you've borrowed them!) A girl can have a certain status among her peers if she has an older brother, especially if he's good looking!

At best, older brothers will protect you from hassle, plead your case with irate parents or bail you out with a pound or two when you're skint. They may bully you a bit and you will have to be tactful about their girlfriends. It's worth the effort though, especially if your brother has passed his driving test and has his own set of wheels!

Bullying

See also
Verbal Abuse

Bullying is very common indeed, at all ages and stages. Most people are bullied to some degree or other at some time during their school life. Sometimes it's a passing thing, especially if you're a fairly confident person to begin with. Not everyone is, however. Unfortunately, it's the nature of a bully to target someone who stands out or is different or vulnerable in some way, and a lot of further damage can be done to a person who is already insecure, lonely or hurt.

Bullies are almost always themselves unhappy and inadequate people. They need to dominate or ridicule others to boost their own low self-esteem. Usually they depend upon their hangers-on to support them. Alone, they become pathetic people.

15

The only way to deal with a bully is to stand up to him or her. You will almost certainly need help to do this. If you're being bullied, *tell someone*; a parent, or a teacher or some other adult who you trust. There may be threats of repercussions, or you may be called a grass, or worse. Take no notice. Teachers usually know the score, and how best to deal with it. Suffering in silence is doing no-one any favours, the bullied person or the bullies themselves. Sadly, people who are persistently bullied sometimes react by themselves picking on someone smaller and weaker. It takes guts to break the cycle, but *it can be done!*

cC

Careers

See *also*
Jobs, Work

Some fortunate people know from an early age the career they want to follow. Most take longer to decide. It's often difficult, especially when decisions have to be taken at the stage of choosing GCSE options and so on.

If you're sure of what you want, go for it. Motivation is perhaps your most positive asset. Never forget though, that academic or vocational success aren't the only things in life. Take time for relaxation, friends, family and fun. Most of all, for your relationship with God. That's the thing that will endure through life and beyond.

If you're not sure of what you want to do, look around at all the possibilities. Despite recessions and unemployment and other depressing things, the world is bursting with opportunities for young people, especially if they're Christians. Maybe this is the most exciting time there's ever been! Don't be afraid to speak to the experts who are there to help you. Ask yourself what really interests you. What you enjoy and find fulfilling. Where you feel you would fit.

Don't panic if you still can't decide or if you think you've chosen the wrong course. You can always change channel. Ask for advice and help if you need it. Pray and ask for God's guidance in your career. He has a perfect plan for your life, just waiting for you to fit into. Enjoy it!

Church

What is the church? Does the word 'church' make you think of that grey stone edifice with a tower or a steeple, that you pass every day on your way to school? Or the Sunday morning service you've gone to with your parents ever since you can remember? Or something else altogether?

Church buildings come in all shapes and sizes, from smart modern buildings to small tin-roofed huts, from community centres to lofty cathedrals, from historic parish churches to village chapels, and lots in between.

Church isn't really about a building at all. The first church members in the days immediately after Jesus had gone back to heaven, had no building but moved about from house to house for their church services. The church is really the company of people who have come to a relationship with Jesus Christ and committed their lives to him. However, most local gatherings of Christians have a place called church where they meet regularly to worship and to share their lives with one another and with God. Christians are not meant to struggle along alone, but to be part of a family, the 'body of Christ' of which he is head.

No family is perfect, and your church won't be perfect either, but each member needs the others, to encourage, to strengthen, to learn from, to correct when needed, to belong to, to enjoy. And Jesus needs his church to make him complete. (Read Acts 2:36-42.)

Clothes
See also **Fashion**

Clothes are much more than a necessary covering or something to keep out the cold.

Clothes make a statement to the world about the kind of person you are.

You're probably happiest in your jeans, tops, jackets and boots, like most people of your age. You may or may not have hassle from your mum, who would like you to dress up now and again, if only to please her. You usually resist, not least because you feel your mother has a very sad taste in clothes. However, she does have some very nice garments in her wardrobe that you don't mind borrowing now and then. It's quite fortunate for you that she's put on a bit of weight and can't borrow yours!

No doubt you feel that you'd like more clothes than you can afford on a very limited budget. Swapping with your friends is a good idea. So are charity shops. It's nice to have lots of options, though it does add to the time spent making that important decision about what to put on each day. Then, at the end of the day you'll probably leave a pile of discarded garments on your bedroom floor and go out in your usual jeans, top and boots!

Complexes

A complex can develop from the most casual of remarks, even something like 'Your hair looks so nice now that you're wearing it up.'

It's possible to take quite the wrong meaning and get the idea that your hair looks terrible worn down rather than up, even to the point where you never leave the house without it pulled back and secured with a battery of hair grips and scrunchy bands.

Try not to read things into comments that were never intended. Some people can be thoughtless in their remarks without meaning any harm. On the other hand, try to build up the confidence of others by saying positive things rather than pulling them down with negatives.

Computers

Computers and wordprocessors are part of most modern teaching equipment, whether it's school, college, university or any training course. Whatever your chosen subjects and goals, you will be expected to be computer literate. Don't let computer games and the Internet take too much of your leisure time, however. A couple of hours in front of a screen can flash past like ten minutes. Thank God for the micro-chip, and use it well.

Conservation

It is to the credit of many young people today that they are concerned with life on our planet and the conservation of its resources. This generation cares about such issues as animal rights and the preservation of the countryside. It minds that the Brazilian rain forests are in danger of disappearing and the balance of nature threatened. It worries about the hole in the ozone layer and is aware of the need for protection from UV rays. It is keen to recycle waste, plant trees, collect for good causes, save whales and campaign against the trapping of animals for their fur, and clean up polluted waterways. It cares about the plight of war and famine victims, the homeless, underprivileged and exploited in our own and other societies.

We had a commission from our Creator God to care for the earth and we have in general failed to carry it out. The greed and carelessness and apathy of mankind have all had a part to play in the disintegration of our world. Ultimately, there will be a new heaven and a new earth. Meanwhile, in the time remaining, may this generation have the will and the courage to go some way towards redeeming the damage done to this present one. (Read Proverbs 8:22-31.)

Cooking

See also
Food, Diets

Cooking is something that everyone should learn, male or female. Never pass up the chance of cookery classes, whether Cordon Bleu or simple basic stuff. They'll pay dividends in later life, maybe when you go to college or university, or to work away from home, not to mention when you have a home of your own.

You'll probably learn anyway, by trial and error or from cookery books, but there are lots of short cuts and little touches that make it all easier and the results more exciting.

Cooking, serving and eating a meal with friends is one of life's pleasures. It's fun to make the table special with candles and flowers and your nicest tableware. Try it as a way of introducing some of your favourite people to each other. Or just for a few old friends. Or even Mum and Dad!

Cousins

Cousins are a strange breed, not quite siblings but not exactly friends either. You can't choose your cousins. They are forced upon you for better or worse, and you can't help meeting them at family gatherings.

Cousins are great when you're all small together. Remember those family occasions when the adults exchanged gossip and put the world to rights, while a horde of cousins rampaged through the house (usually Grandma's) creating glorious havoc? Later, the older boy cousins grew long of leg and hoarse of voice, and the girls tended to blush easily and giggle a lot. Later still, they began to drift off to college, and return strangely grown-up and sophisticated. Never mind. They'll always be your cousins. And don't worry too much about being compared to that annoyingly pretty or clever cousin – it's just another irritating habit of the parent generation!

Cults
See also **Religions**

There are plenty of cults, sects and strange teachings around in this day and age, and sometimes it's difficult to sort out what's what. The fact that many Christians now meet in house groups, small fellowships and enquirer's groups, cell units and so on, makes it doubly confusing, especially for parents who justifiably worry about just what it is their children may be getting into. Their anxiety is understandable.

If you are a young Christian whose parents are concerned about you, the best way to reassure them is to invite them along to see just exactly what goes on in your particular youth club, Alpha group, or whatever else you may be involved in as part of your church life. All genuine leaders would welcome that kind of parental interest, and most have parents' evenings or special events when everyone can get to know each other.

Avoid like the plague any gathering that meets in secret, or encourages you to break away from your family, or to actively rebel against the rules and guidelines laid down by parents and those in authority. Whatever they call themselves, these groups are not likely to be centred around Jesus.

As far as sound teaching goes, perhaps the most important question to ask is whether Jesus Christ is worshipped and acknowledged as the Son of God and the only means by which we can come into a right relationship with God. All true teaching must be centred around that. (Read Matthew 7:15-23.)

Death

See also
Eternal Life

No one likes to think about death. Most of us when we're young tend to think that it will never happen to us. It's perhaps only when we lose someone close to us, a precious grandfather or grandmother or a friend, or someone is killed in an accident, that we have to stop and face the fact of death.

Physical death happens to us all. It could be sooner or later; we don't know and it's good that we don't. We do not, however, need to live our lives in the shadow of the fear of death, which is spoken of in the Bible. Jesus came to deliver us from that shadow, so that we can live our lives in happy security.

We are told very clearly that anyone who knows and loves God will never die. Their body will perish but the real, vital person that we are will live on into a glorious eternity with God, where we will know happiness beyond our wildest dreams. Our destination after death can be settled now by trusting in Jesus. (Read 1 Corinthians 15:22.)

Decision Making

There are many decisions that have to be made in life. Perhaps the first big thing you'll have to decide is which subjects to take and which to drop at the beginning of your GCSE years. Then there'll be decisions about further study, colleges, the choice of a career and of a life partner, your family and your lifestyle and many more. Decisions have to be made at every stage of life, and sometimes it's hard to make the right one. Friends and family can help. Even better, ask God to guide you at every stage where a decision has to be made.

Depression

See also **Hormones**

Depression can hit at any age. Most people are depressed at some time or other. Developing hormones can make for very up and down feelings in your teenage years. The odd down day is nothing to worry about and you'll probably feel different tomorrow.

On the other hand, depression that goes on and on, whether for a reason or not, could mean you need help. Loss of appetite, insomnia, anxiety and hopelessness are symptoms that you should seek help for, from your doctor, a trusted friend, a parent or someone at church. Help is available, take what is offered, trust God and you will come through to laugh and enjoy life again.

Diets

See also
Cooking, Food, Eating Disorders

A balanced diet is essential for proper growth and development, clear skin, healthy hair, alertness and energy. Daily intake of food should include proteins, carbohydrates, fats, minerals and vitamins.

Crash diets are not a good idea. These put a strain on the body, the weight loss is put back quite quickly and the repeated yo-yo effect of weight loss and gain creates extra strain. A wiser course of action is to develop a healthy pattern of eating, including items from all the essential groups above. Eat plenty of fresh foods – salads, fresh fruit, vegetables, wholegrain cereals and bread. If you've opted for being a vegetarian, be sure to include lots of pulses, cheese, eggs and whole milk.

Skipping meals is not a good idea, especially breakfast. Neither is stuffing onself with junk food – crisps, chocolate, burgers and chips – though all of these are OK in moderation. Try exercise as an alternative to dieting if you're not happy with your figure. Walking, jogging, cycling, swimming, aerobics – all help to tone and condition the body as well as burning up excess calories. Eating is one of the great pleasures of life, especially a meal in the company of good friends. Thank God for the enormous range of available foods we have, and choose well from them.

Divorce

Divorce, sadly, is a fact of life in the age we live in. An increasingly high percentage of marriages are ending in divorce and broken homes.

God intended marriage to be for a lifetime, the loving commitment of a man and a woman to stay together for mutual support, comfort, sharing and enjoyment and to bring up the children of their marriage in love and security.

We live in an imperfect world, all men and women are faulty beings, and this ideal all too often breaks down, even, sadly, in Christian families. Divorce hurts everyone, not least the children. There are no winners. If your parents are divorced, you will have suffered because of it. It would be pointless to pretend otherwise.

But if you are a Christian, the love of Jesus in your life can make all the difference. Whichever parent was at fault, wherever you feel your sympathies lie, ask God to help you forgive them both. Resentment and bitterness do nothing but spoil your own life. Your parents are both hurting people and need your love and your forgiveness. Don't shut either of them out.

Apart from God, the pattern of broken marriage and divorce will often repeat itself in the next generation. With God, the pattern can be broken. All things are made new. With Christ at the centre of your life, you have every chance of meeting the life partner of his choice and achieving a happy and lasting marriage.

Doubt

We all have doubts. Doubt about our own worth, our abilities, our relationships, our future, just about everything. Even about God.

The strongest Christian has probably doubted God at some time or other. Doubted his ability to sort out an impossible situation, doubted that he really cares about us, or knows us, or answers our prayers, Doubted that he exists at all.

It's OK to have doubts. Don't pretend to be full of faith and confidence if you're not. Find a trusted older person, maybe in your family or at church, and talk to them about your doubts. Best of all, be honest with God and tell him about your doubts too.

Dreams

Dreams are strange things. Everyone dreams, whenever they sleep, though they may not remember. Sleep experts reckon that dreams are necessary for our psychological and emotional health.

Some dreams may be strange or disturbing. Some may be astonishingly clear in detail. God sometimes uses dreams to tell someone something he wants them to know. If you feel this is the case, ask him what he is telling you.

Don't worry if nothing comes of it. Dreams can't hurt you. An upsetting one is probably just the result of that late snack of cheese on toast that you ate before bed!

Drugs

There are different types of drugs. Drugs are natural or chemical substances which, used under medical supervision, can treat chemical imbalance and other conditions and illnesses. Unfortunately, drugs are also subject to abuse which has become more widespread among young people. Deaths, chronic illness, ruined relationships and spoiled potential of young lives has resulted.

Drugs can stimulate or depress the nervous system, produce delusions or hallucinations or feelings of euphoria, block out reality and even create the ability to perform unusual physical feats such as dancing non-stop for many hours.

The immediate danger is overdose, usually resulting in psychosis, convulsions, coma and even death. Drug users are liable to become dependent and long term abuse can destroy a healthy body and mind. Users are liable to organ damage, malnutrition, mental illness, hepatitis, HIV and other infections.

It's best to strictly avoid drugs, however harmless they may appear and however socially acceptable you might be encouraged to believe the habit is.

If you're a Christian, pray for your friends who may be tempted into drug taking. Be filled with the Holy Spirit who brings real joy and fulfilment and show the world there's an alternative to the sad delusion of drugs.

eE

Eating Disorders

See also **Diets**

There is a great deal of pressure these days for girls to have the 'ideal' figure, which unfortunately seems to mean thin.

We are all different builds and sizes. There is no ideal. If you are an average weight for your height and build and you feel well, don't be manipulated by pressure from the media or anywhere else.

Anorexia and Bulimia Nervosa are commonly known as Slimmer's Disease. This is misleading. Both these disorders are the outward sign of something desperately wrong inside. Anorexics continue to lose weight through restricting food intake even when long past the point of acceptable slimness. Bulimics eat normally and then vomit up the food they've eaten. Sometimes they binge on large amounts before vomiting, and may use laxatives too. Acid from the stomach can seriously damage the digestive system, throat and teeth. Both anorexics and bulimics face a grave danger to life.

The underlying problem is the thing that needs to be tackled. People with eating disorders need the will to want to get better. Recovery takes time.

If you feel you may have an eating disorder or are concerned for a friend, seek help. Be honest, face facts, pray and know that God cares and can help.

Embarrassment

So many things in life can be the source of embarrassment. Like teachers, or boys, or blushing, or families. Actually, *especially* families!

Families will behave in an embarrassing way when you take a new friend home for tea, for instance. Your little sister will giggle, your dad will blow his nose in that peculiar honking way, your grandma will insist on talking about you when you were a baby or even worse, when your dad was a baby! Your brother's eating habits embarrass you, and so does the sad and strange outfit your mother has decided to wear. Even the dog will embarrass you by sniffing at your friend's ankles . . . or worse!

Going shopping with your mum is a mega-embarrassment. It's not just the sad outfit (another one), it's her whole attitude. She doesn't know it's uncool to hold up dresses against you, or comment on them, or come into the changing room with you. She can't grasp that all she's required to do is wait quietly by the door and come forward with the cheque book when she's needed!

Seriously, embarrassment is common, but it loses its edge in time. Your confidence will grow and you'll gain assurance. You'll probably even stop blushing in time!

Eternal Life
See also **Death**

Eternal life is God's gift to mankind which is freely available to us when we accept his son Jesus Christ as our Saviour and Lord.

It's hard to imagine a life that goes on forever, with no time span, no limitations, no end. A life that is not bounded by physical problems, or social issues or space or need of any kind. It's mind boggling! But it's what we can look forward to when this life is over, and you have to admit, that's fairly amazing!

The fear of death is something that hangs over every person ever born, to a greater or lesser degree. Whatever we achieve or gain in this life, will come to an end one day. As an old song says, 'You can't take it with you when you go'.

Even our bodies will be left behind, like a garment we discard because we've outgrown it or it's worn out. But the real 'us', the personality which makes us who we are, goes on for ever.

We're not given many details of what we can expect in the next life. We read a few tantalising hints that there will be 'pleasures for evermore' and 'fullness of joy'. We will meet again loved ones who have died and we will see Jesus face to face.

Eternal life in heaven will be much more wonderful, fulfilling and joyful than anything our limited minds can imagine, and it all begins here and now. We are told that, in Jesus, we know that we have eternal life.

Evil

See also **Sin**

The world is a bad place, and appears to be getting worse. Every day our newspapers and TV screens bear witness to the terrible things that go on. We do not need to detail them but we all have to admit that it's true.

The scene blackens. The Bible says that in the world, the forces of evil will get worse and worse, until the time of the Lord's return.

Hopeless? A case for deep despair? No. The Bible also says that Jesus is the light of the world. All of us who belong to him are walking in the light, and that the light will overcome the darkness. Let your light shine!

Exams

Exams are nerve-racking occasions, whatever their level. The build up to them, the reading, the feverish revision, the striving to remember information that might be relevant, is equally stressful. Add to this the fact that many exams are held in early summer, peak times for hay fever, and it's a wonder that anyone ever passes anything!

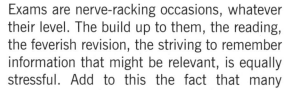

You can minimise the strain. Be sure to eat proper meals at regular times, not snacks at midnight. Get plenty of sleep. (Midnight revison is not a good idea anyway.) Get some fresh air and exercise. Do your best on the day, but let God be in charge of the outcome, whatever it turns out to be. What matters is that you do your best . . . and relax!

Faith

Faith is something we all have a bit of. We use faith in all kinds of situations in everyday life, without even thinking about it. We have faith that a chair will bear our weight when we sit on it or that water will come out when we turn on the tap.

Faith in God is more difficult to define, because we can't see God, but we all have a little of that sort of faith, too. The Bible tells us that each of us is given a measure of faith. It's what we do with it that counts. Choosing to believe in Jesus, to take him at his word, will enable our faith to grow. The more we have faith, the more faith we have. (Read Hebrews 11:1-16.)

Families

See *also*
Father, Mother, Brothers, Sisters, Cousins, Grandparents, Parents

Families can be sheer torture when you're young. From being a comforting, safe, pre-dictable kind of people-group (if you're lucky), they can change almost overnight. Suddenly, your mother nags and worries and your father fumes and yells. Your older brother makes hurtful remarks about your appearance, your sister gets spiteful and your smaller siblings become pests. Even your grandparents have a tendency to lecture you. Small wonder that you often burst into tears and rush out of the room.

What happened? Things were OK before so why has everyone in the family suddenly changed?

Families

Maybe, just maybe, they haven't changed that much. It's more likely to be down to hormones . . . yours! You're not a child anymore but not quite an adult. In between is a confusing place to be. It's confusing for you, and for everyone else in your family too. There's one comfort though. Give your family members a year or two and you'll probably find they all grow out of it!

Fashion

See also
Clothes, Boots

Fashions come and go. Often they come and go very fast indeed! Your mother may tell you she wore the same thing 25 years ago, but you are unlikely to be impressed with the limp garment she pulls from the back of the wardrobe.

Fashion is what hangs in racks in the high street boutiques, and is being worn by everyone now, but the best fashion is your own. Don't be led by the crowd!

Father

Every girl needs a father. A father is meant to be provider, protector, friend, defender, model of a man, comforter and (sometimes) judge. A father looks out for your interests at all times, and a good father would lay down his life for his child.

Not all fathers measure up to this ideal. Human fathers are, well, *human*. Some fathers are dysfunctional or absent. Some fathers never had fathers themselves and some fathers fail through no fault of their own.

God is the father who never fails. He understands and loves each of his children unconditionally, whatever our situation, whatever our background, whatever we have done. He is the father of those who have good human fathers and particularly, he is the father of the fatherless. (Read Psalm 127.)

Fear

Everyone has to cope with fear in one form or another. Fears range from nagging anxieties about your friendships, your future or something you have done, to fears about your family splitting up, fears of illness and fear of death. There are even the seemingly insignificant ones like fear of spiders or of the dark. Fears that seriously limit our everyday lives could be described as neuroses or phobias. There are experts who can help us deal with these extreme fears.

Most fears can be overcome by bringing them out into the open and talking about them. Discuss your worries with someone you know and trust. If you go to church or a youth group, get someone to pray with you. Fears seem to grow smaller when they are shared, and the chances are they'll shrink away altogether and disappear.

Figure
See **Bras**

Football
See also **Games**

You either love football or you loathe it. It's not everyone's idea of a brilliant weekend, shivering in the stands amidst a crowd of cheering, jeering, hollering, fanatical football fans. On the other hand, if you've been brought up with a dad/brothers/cousins who are avid supporters of a team, you'll probably be the most fanatical spectator of all.

Forgiveness

We need to forgive and we need to be forgiven – the two things go together. We have forgiveness because Jesus took the punishment for our sins when he died on the cross. But we may still need to confess and ask forgiveness each time we are aware we have done wrong. Then, as far as God is concerned, it's all forgotten.

Forgiveness between fellow humans is important too. We may need to ask forgiveness of one another if we have said or done something we know to be wrong and hurtful. It may simply be because our attitude is wrong or that we've made a mistake. A sincere apology is the best way of melting away bad feeling and resentment. In the same way, we need to forgive others who have hurt or harmed us. Holding on to a grudge or seeking revenge will harm ourselves more than it harms the other person. There's freedom to be gained in letting go of anger and grudges.

On the other hand, forgiveness doesn't necessarily mean that we must put ourselves in the position where we can be hurt in the same way again.

Food

See also

Cooking, Diets, Eating Disorders

Food is one of the great enjoyments of life, to be used well and wisely. We in the West have a great variety of food to choose from. Sadly, much of it is the 'junk' variety; fastfood, takeaways, instant frozen foods. All convenient and time-saving, in moderation, but let's not forget to balance our diet with plenty of fresh foods, fruit, veg and salads, wholegrains, and freshly prepared home-cooked food. Healthy eating is a good habit to get into and is cheaper as well. That's not to say we can't pig out occasionally, but better not to make a habit of it!

We can be thankful for the quality and abundance of our foods, but we mustn't be greedy or wasteful, bearing in mind that a great proportion of the world's people don't have enough to eat.

g G

Games

See also **Football**

You may or may not be interested in traditional games of the sports variety, i.e. tennis, netball, hockey. If you are, great! Sport is a terrific way of keeping fit, functioning as part of a team, making friends and working off surplus energy. If you're not sporty, don't worry, there are plenty of other people like you. You're probably into computer games or cyberpets.

As for board and card games (Chess, Monopoly, Trivial Pursuit, Pictionary, etc) they may seem completely uncool but it's surprising how much fun they can be.

Going Out

See also
Relationships,
Boyfriends

'Going out' in your parents' day meant getting ready, being picked up or meeting at a certain time, actually going somewhere and arriving home (probably at a set time).

Nowadays, going out seems to be less defined. It can be spending time, or hanging out with a special person, or, it can mean that you have a certain kind of understanding with someone. It's a good idea to sort out what the expectations are before you agree to 'go out' with someone.

God

Undoubtedly the most important decision you'll have to make concerns your personal relationship with God. You may or may not have grown up with people who believe in God and have committed their lives to him. Either way, you'll have to make up your own mind. Most people have thoughts about God that they may or may not share with others.

If you're searching for God, don't be afraid to ask. Speak to people you know are involved with church or youth groups. Read books. Find out other people's experiences. Ask questions. Best of all, try speaking to God for yourself, even if you're not quite sure about him. Tell him whatever is on your mind. He's not very far away and will be delighted to hear from you.

Grandparents

Grandparents are sometimes a pain, but can also be the biggest assets in the world. Grandparents are not directly responsible for you, therefore their attitude is fairly laid-back. Grandparents enjoy spoiling you with treats and presents when you are small, and slipping you a fiver for something special when you are older. Grandparents brag about your accomplishments, turn a blind eye to your failings and laugh indulgently at your escapades (although your parents probably see that the very worst are kept from them). They beam with pride at your school-plays, prize-givings and graduations, and boast about you in public to the point of embarrassment.

Grandparents may be elderly but they can be surprisingly understanding, tolerant or even broad-minded. They don't shock as easily as you might expect. They've got a lot of living under their belt and they're likely to have seen it all before.

Groups
See **Youth Groups**

hH

Hair

Can anything on earth be worse than a bad hair day? If your style refuses to settle, your ends are split or you've got a fit of the frizzies, it can blight the sunniest morning or dampen the brightest mood. Some days, no amount of washing, conditioning, blowing and styling can make your hair look the way you want it too.

We all get those days. Maybe though we're the only ones who notice how awful our hair is. Possibly it's not even as awful as all that. A good diet is a must for healthy hair. So is regular washing in mild shampoo (too often or too harsh products will strip hair of its natural oils), a good cut and a style that suits you. Deep conditioning treatment will help dryness, and is not too expensive – you can get a sachet for around a pound.

Fashionable styles come and go, but one head of hair is all you'll get, so it pays to take care of it!

Health

We're fortunate in having one of the best health services in the world and all for free during school and student years. Good habits lay down a sound basis for a healthy life. It's cool to eat the right food, have vaccinations, medical and dental checks, and be aware of the dangers of alcohol and drug abuse, and sexually transmitted diseases. Everyone needs some kind of exercise and enough sleep. Good habits started early can go a long way towards ensuring a lifetime of good health.

Holidays
See *also* **Travel**

Holidays can be fantastic fun or they can be the pits. It depends a lot on what you make of them. You can be miserable in Miami or have a great time in Great Yarmouth.

Maybe the best holidays are when you're with a group your own age with similar interests. Christian camps, house parties, youth conferences, even summer mission outreach, can be among the most rewarding and amazing times of your life. You'll strengthen existing friendships, make rewarding new ones, and probably find you book up straight away for next year.

Family holidays can be a bit more tricky, especially when there's a wide diversity of age groups. You may feel bored or restricted if there are people much older or much younger than you to be considered. Try not to moan too much. Your mum wants you to be happy and is probably working her socks off to make sure all of you have a good time. You might even find that you do!

Holy Spirit

The Holy Spirit is the third person of the trinity. He is the spirit of Jesus, sent by him after he had ascended back to his father in Heaven. The Holy Spirit comes to live within every believer when they commit themselves to God through faith in Jesus Christ.

The Holy Spirit is likened to fire, wind, oil, water, and a dove. He came with great power at the first Pentecost and transformed the lives of the first Christians. He is available in the same way to transform lives today.

Any Christian can receive this filling of the Holy Spirit by asking for it. It can be helpful to do this within a group of mature and trusted Christians. We read in the Bible that the spirit-filled Christian bears fruit in his or her life; love, joy, peace, patience, kindness, goodness, faithfulness, humility and self-control. The Holy Spirit also gives the gifts of wisdom, knowledge, faith, healing, miracle working, prophecy, tongues and interpretation, to be used for the benefit of others as well as the recipient.

The Holy Spirit can be grieved if we reject him in our lives, and his working can be quenched if we do not obey.
(Read 1 Corinthians 14:13-20.)

Home
See also **Families**

There is an old saying that home is the place where you behave your worst and are treated the best. Maybe it's not far wrong. In a good home, you will feel free to let your hair down, show your feelings, freak out if you need to, just be yourself. You can't pull the wool over the eyes of the people you live with anyway. You will be tolerated and forgiven in a way that would happen nowhere else.

Home is another institution that is largely what you make it. It can be a haven or it can be hell on earth. We do well to thank God for our homes and make them the best we possibly can.

Homework

It's a drag, isn't it? And possibly the last thing you feel like doing after a hard day at school. All you want to do is relax, see friends, watch TV, listen to music or just crash out. It's a necessary evil though, and best tackled and got out of the way as soon as possible, maybe after a meal and a short rest. Your conscience is then clear and you have a bit of time to yourself. Storing up weekend homework for a last frantic effort on Sunday evening is not a good idea either.

Hormones

See also
Depression, Periods

Hormones are responsible for a great deal of aggro during your teenage years. The onset of puberty, with its release of hormones into the bloodstream, is responsible for the normal body changes as you become an adult. This process can also be blamed for mood changes, tiredness, hyperactivity, and other ups and downs. All this is normal and things will settle down again before too long. You are not going through a personality change, and neither are the people around you, though it may be a difficult time for everyone.

Unfortunately, hormone activity in a teenage girl can sometimes coincide with the other end of the scale for a mother approaching menopause. Both need a little extra TLC, tact and understanding, and maybe your own space and privacy from time to time.

Hypocrisy

This generation is probably somewhat less hypocritical than some of those that have gone before. You are not afraid to ask questions and demand answers, you do not put on an act to please your elders, and you will not suffer those who say one thing and do another.

As regards your faith in God, you will not be satisfied with something handed down from your parents, but must find and experience truth for yourself.

All this is to your credit, and God will honour those who are honest with him and with themselves. However, please don't be too harsh with those who don't know all the answers or who seem to fall short in some way. The most sincere and mature Christians are only human and can make mistakes now and then. (Read Matthew 21:28-32.)

il

Ideals

It's easy to be idealistic, to see things in terms of black and white, right and wrong. Our ideals don't always coincide with those of our parents' generation, however. We need to have ideals, something to aim for and attain to. It's probable though that our sights will change as we grow older, that black and white changes to shades of grey, that some of our ideals are impossible to realise. Disillusionment can set in, but with God in our lives we can acknowledge our own weakness and allow him to work his purposes in us and for us.

Idols

Idols don't have to be statues, images or carved figures. They can also be pop stars, boyfriends, a prized possession, or our own ambition – anything that takes the place of God in our lives. Anything can be an idol if we let it. God's word states very clearly that he must take first place in our lives and, like all his commands, that this is for our own good.

Individual

See *also*
Peer Pressure

There's a lot of pressure to follow the trend, to be part of the crowd. It stems from a basic need to be accepted and loved. We need to remind ourselves that God has created us as

Individual

individual beings. No two are exactly alike. There's never been another person exactly like you in the world's history, and there never will be. You are a unique individual, a one-off. God broke the mould when he made you. So, let's not try too hard to be like everyone else, or even like anyone else. Let's rejoice in the things we have in common and in our differences too.

Jealousy

Jealousy is a real nasty! It nags away at your mind, ties your stomach into knots and generally messes up your life. Maybe you're jealous of a brother or sister who you think gets more time/attention/privileges than you do? Or of someone your age who is prettier, or cleverer, or who attracts the guys who don't seem to notice you at all?

Being jealous is a dead loss and a real waste of time and energy. It doesn't get you anywhere and gives you a load of ugly, spiteful, negative feelings you're better off without. The person you're jealous of has probably got plenty of problems and hang-ups too. They may even be jealous of you!

Friendships and family relationships are, humanly speaking, probably the most important things in life. Don't let them be spoiled by jealousy. (Read Psalm 37.)

Jesus

Jesus Christ is the central figure of the whole Christian faith. He is part of the trinity of

Father, Son and Holy Spirit. He is fully God, yet he became human and lived an ordinary life on earth in order to share our experiences, our joys and sorrows and sufferings. He died on the cross to take the punishment for our sins, so that we can go free. He rose from the dead so that we can have victory over death. He went back to his father in heaven, and sent us his spirit to fill us and help us in our lives.

He is described as our saviour, priest, prophet, friend, king, and husband! He loves us all and wants us to be with him for eternity. Isn't that amazing!

Jobs

See also
Careers, Work

It's good to have a Saturday or holiday job. You learn a bit about what it's like to go to work, and get a lot of experience of dealing with people and working alongside others. You may even land up with something that helps you decide on your future career (even if it's something you find you definitely *don't* want to do!) Best of all, you'll have some cash of your own and won't have to be so dependent on stingy pocket-money and hand-outs from hard-up parents!

Kissing

Kissing can be a great worry (that is, kissing a boy) especially if you haven't done much (or any) of it before. The simple snog seems fraught with problems. Who should you kiss? How exactly do you do it? How long should a kiss last? What does it mean? What happens to the noses?

Don't worry about it. Kissing is no big deal, and there's no formula for doing it. You could practice by puckering the lips in front of a mirror but you'll waste a lot of time and won't gain much. A kiss with someone you trust and are genuinely fond of will happen spontaneously when the time is right.

Late Nights

You probably get an awful lot of hassle about late nights. Everyone wants to stay out as late as their friends do, and think it's unreasonable of parents to object. Don't they understand you'll be just fine?

The trouble is, they don't. To a teenager, parents are hopelessly out of touch, their idea of a late night being to stay up until 11.30 pm watching a TV film with a mug of cocoa. However, they object because they care. They're concerned not only for your safety but for your health, your wellbeing, your happiness and your future. That's why they make rules. Try and talk it over and come to an agreement that's acceptable to all parties. And thank God, for parents who care.

Letters

See *also* **Privacy**

Do you ever get that awful feeling that your mum might be sneakily reading your letters, steaming them open and sticking them down again? Do you keep your mail firmly under lock and key, out of the way of younger siblings? Do you have a hunch your dad holds your letters up to the light to try and decipher the handwriting within?

Relax! Most people – even families – respect the right of another's privacy, and probably wouldn't find the contents as interesting as you think, in any case. Anyway, the more secretive you are, the more they'll think you have something to hide. Be cool with your correspondence.

Lending

There are two sides to lending. It's a great drag when your younger sister wants to borrow your new top, or your bike, or your make-up, or your latest CD. You know without any doubt it'll come back creased, or damaged, or used up, or scratched. Or not come back at all!

On the other hand, it seems perfectly reasonable to borrow your big brother's new shirt, or his bike, or his razor, or his new video. And he really doesn't need to be such a pain, complaining that it's crumpled, or dented, or damaged, or mislaid . . .

Loneliness

It's possible to be lonely even in the middle of a crowd. It's lonely when people aren't on your wavelength, like when you're the only Christian in your year. It's lonely when you're revising for exams and everyone else seems to be out enjoying themselves. It's lonely when you feel misunderstood. It's lonely when you move to a new home, or a new school, or a new situation and don't know anyone, and everyone else seems to fit into some tight little group. Even family holidays can be lonely, when there's no one else your age to talk to.

Wallowing in self-pity doesn't really help. Why not look for someone else who might be lonely too and make the first move towards getting to know them?

Love

Love is . . .

Well, it's many things. It's growing up in a warm, close family who care for you. It's finding a special friend of either sex, with whom you have things in common, who you trust and who you know will always be there for you. It's meeting that special person and experiencing those heart-stopping, stomach-churning, spine-tingling, pulse-quickening emotions that are associated with falling in love. It's getting to know someone, finding that you 'click' in the way you think, or view the world, or laugh at things. It's learning to care, and especially to care as much about the other person's needs as about your own. It's being secure enough to be able to reach out and love others without being afraid of getting hurt ourselves. Love is belonging. Perhaps the best description of love is given in the New Testament: I Corinthians 13.

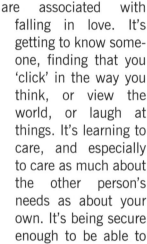

m**M**

Magazines

The bookstalls are full of magazines specially designed for the teenage girl. Generally speaking, they're a mix of true-life confession-type stories, cartoons, music and fashion features, readers letters, and agony-aunt advice on health, family problems, personal worries, school and relationships. Mostly they lean heavily towards boy/girl concerns. Teen magazines try to reflect life as it is, and on the whole, make an effort to be responsible. But take care. The majority don't represent a Christian world-view. There are some excellent Christian mags about though. They're worth looking out for. Most of them are fairly with-it and bang up-to-date, and can be a real help in maintaining Christian standards in the difficult real world.

Make-up

Your mother probably tells you that you don't need to use make-up as you have a young skin, a fresh complexion, good colouring, etc.

You just know that you need every bit of help you can get to disguise your all-too-apparent faults, or to improve on what God saw fit to hand out to you in the way of looks.

Make-up can't work miracles, but it sure can help! It's a bit sad to slap it on with a trowel, though. Better to find out what suits you, your colouring and skin-type. A makeover can be a good laugh, maybe with a friend to share it as a birthday treat. You'll come out feeling like a million dollars, your confidence will get a boost and you'll probably learn a lot too. But always remember – it's not the make-up that makes you beautiful but *who you are*! (Corny, but true!)

Marriage

See also
Weddings

The idea of marriage can produce mixed feelings. Many young people today feel that marriage is outdated and that it's a commitment impossible to maintain. After all, the sad fact is that at least one out of three marriages today ends in divorce.

There's arguably no such thing as a perfect marriage, but it's an ideal worth striving for and working towards. God sets a high value upon marriage, likening it to the union between Christ and his body. The Church of England wedding service states that the purposes of marriage are for mutual care, comfort and encouragement, and to provide a secure environment for the nurture and upbringing of children.

There is no doubt that a secure, committed marriage, even one with faults, is the best setting for raising children to be stable and balanced individuals. Like any other institution, a marriage will go through change, growth and neccessary adjustment as it matures. There needs to be flexibility, tolerance, kindness and plenty of humour, but a good marriage can last a lifetime and be the greatest blessing of all.

Mistakes

See also
Reputation

Everyone makes mistakes. Some don't matter (though usually we could kick ourselves at the time). Others can have far-reaching consequences. Once a mistake is made, it usually can't be reversed. But we can react positively from our mistakes by learning from them, and, hopefully, by not making the same mistake twice.

Mother

It's said that the most intense relationship in the human experience is that of a mother and her daughter. It could well be true. The daughter's growing-up time can be traumatic for both. A mother wants to protect her daughter from the heartaches she may have suffered herself. A daughter is determined to go her own way and make her own mistakes. A mother sometimes resents the fact (maybe subconsciously) that her daughter is growing into an attractive woman, while a daughter feels that her mother thinks she knows everything.

Mothers and daughters can be good friends, but they can also have spectacular rows, the kind of screaming matches that send the menfolk heading for the door.

Things will settle down and even out. You will probably discover that you have a lot in common. A daughter dreads growing up to be like her mother, but by the time she does, the two of them will probably be the best of friends.

Money

Most of us feel we could do with a bit more money. There's never quite enough for all we feel we need or want, to buy or to do.

It's good to have a way of earning some money, from a Saturday job, or baby-sitting, or even helping out in extra ways at home. Making a little bit of money go a long way can be a challenge and it can be good fun too. Charity shops, jumble sales, car boot sales, are all good hunting grounds. And when you're tired of the possessions you have, you could always get together with friends and have your own sale. It's also rewarding to give something away, however little, to a charity or to someone in need. Give it a try, you could be pleasantly surprised.

Moods
See **Hormones**

Music

Music is important. Whether you're into rock, or classical, instrumental, country and western or jazz, your music fulfils a need and expresses feelings that can't find expression in any other way.

You probably find that your parents' taste in music is seriously sad. By the same token, they wince and reach for the ear-plugs when you're playing your latest CD. Parents' eardrums seem to be hypersensitive, or maybe they're just damaged!

It's a good idea to keep your most reverberating thumping rhythms for sometime other than when they're having forty winks, or the neighbours round for a quiet chat, or watching a weepy on TV.

Moving

Moving home is one of the most traumatic happenings of life. It can be fun, challenging and stimulating, settling into a new home, new school, new church, making new friends and meeting new people.

It can also be a painful pulling-up of roots, leaving special mates or beloved grandparents, being forced to mix with people who speak, work and worship differently, finding your way about a new neighbourhood and learning to fit in.

Moving isn't always easy, but you will adjust and find your feet. Joining something like an evening class, a sports club or youth fellowship, is a good start.

n**N**

Nail-Biting

We'd all love to have long, glossy, lacquered, well-shaped fingernails. Those stumpy, bitten, miserable little appendages to fingers owned by nail-biters, do spoil the image.

Nail-biting is usually a nervous thing, worse in times of stress. You may have the will-power to abstain for a while, but sudden anxiety or some major pressure point can have you reducing those hopefully sprouting nails to their former sad, chewed, down-to-the-quick state in no time.

Painting the nails with a nasty-tasting substance can help. It at least reminds you of what you are doing. Invest in a stunning new shade of nail lacquer or pin up a picture of a beautiful pair of hands complete with long, strong, unbitten nails, and make them your model.

Names

Who doesn't at some time or other, hate the name they were landed with by their well-meaning parents? Who were they to decide, anyway? I mean, how could they tell we were going to grow into a Victoria or an Elizabeth but not a Carly or a Cleo or a Kate?

On the other hand, they had to name us *something* and couldn't very well keep addressing us as 'hey, you!' until we were old enough to choose our own name. So they probably did the best they could in the circumstances.

Most of us get used to our names or even grow attached to them in time. Even if we really hate our name, it can usually be shortened or adapted in some way to suit our taste. Many of us have the added bonus (or burden) of a nickname, anyway.

Nerves

See also
Depression, Fear

Nearly everyone suffers from some degree of 'nerves' at certain times, such as important exams, interviews, taking part in plays or performances, facing new situations or meeting new people. Nerves can affect us with just a necessary flow of extra adrenalin to help us perform, or they can cause horrid stomach-knotting, trembling, paralysing feelings.

Some form of relaxation is good for someone suffering badly from nerves. Allow plenty of time to get ready for the event so that you don't have to rush. Don't forget to eat, even if you feel you couldn't swallow a mouthful. Try to take a few minutes to breathe deeply. Pray about the problem, and ask someone else to pray for you too.

Normal

What is normal? Is there such a thing?

Many people have unnecessary worries about what is normal and what isn't. God has created us with such a diversity of looks, sizes, colours, shapes, abilities, personalities, talents and characterisation that it's almost impossible to describe a norm. Something that is unacceptable in one culture may be perfectly acceptable in another and considered normal.

Christian standards of normality are often different from those of the world. If you are worried, talk to someone you trust who is maybe older and more experienced. And remember, whatever your differences, the chances are that you are every bit as normal as anyone else.

Occult

Meddling with the occult is dangerous, and should be avoided at all costs, however exciting it may seem. The word 'Occult' simply means 'hidden', and we are commanded by God to have nothing to do with the hidden works of darkness. Even things which may seem harmless fun – fortune tellers, horoscopes or playing with Ouija boards – can be dangerous, so the best advice is simply to leave well alone.

Ozone Layer
See **Conservation**

Panic

See also **Nerves**

'Don't panic!' is easy to say but not so easy to put into practice when you're faced with a sudden danger or situation that makes your mouth go dry, your heart race and your arms and legs feel paralysed and frozen to the spot. It might be real danger or it might be the unexpected sight of someone who's just broken your heart, out with his new girlfriend, or it could be anything in between. A few deep breaths will calm you. If you feel faint, clench your fists half a dozen times to return blood to the brain and sit down.

Parents

See also
Mother and Father

Parents can be a mixed blessing. A person in their teens will probably have more confrontations with a parent/parents than anyone else.

They seem to exist solely to prevent you from doing/going/wearing the things/places/ gear you wish to. They don't give you credit for any common sense, intelligence or integrity. They don't understand what it is to be young.

On the other hand, it's worth reflecting that parents are also the people who feed, clothe, house, educate, nurse and nurture you, and pay the telephone bill. Above all, they care. And they go on caring, no matter how much grief you give them. They have feelings. They may not be cool, but parents are people too. (Read Genesis 20:12)

Parties

We all love parties. Or do we? At a party we can, relax, get to know new people, have a laugh and generally chill out. A good party has food and drink, interesting people, music and fun.

The down side is that parties can be scary if you don't know many other people, or if you feel you're not trendy enough, or if you think people might laugh at you when you get up to dance. And at some parties there may be pressure to drink too much, do drugs, or engage in sexual activity. That kind of party is bad news and best avoided.

Having your friends around to party the night away while your parents are out or away is not too clever either. You'll be stressed out trying to keep things under control, and it's hardly worth the music you'll have to face when they find out.

Peer Pressure

See also **Individual**

When everyone else is doing something or going somewhere, it's very tough to be the only one who's not. Each of us needs to belong and to feel accepted as part of the crowd. It's no fun standing outside looking in.

So peer pressure is a strong influence, not to be underestimated. Many a person has given in against their better judgement, whether the pressure is about drugs, alcohol, premarital sex, dishonesty or any number of other things that may seem attractive but are ultimately destructive. Nor can we assume that those people who pressured us will stand by us and support us when we begin to suffer the consequences of our actions. Sadly, they're likely to be the first to desert us and add insult to injury by talking about us behind our backs.

God doesn't intend us to stand alone, or to fight major battles all on our own. He knows it's hard to be a young Christian in today's hostile world. There are others facing the same pressures and together, we can be strong enough to overcome. The Bible says that we are to encourage one another, pray for each other, and bear one another's burdens. (Read Galatians 6:1-2.)

Periods

Periods are a pain, and that's not meant to be a joke. Those times of the month used to be called 'the curse', and it's not hard to understand why! It's a drag having to spend time being moody, tired, out-of-sorts and prone to all kinds of physical ills from stomach cramps to spots. Having to postpone meaningful life for days every single month is just not fair! Guys just don't know how lucky they are!

There are all kinds of things available to help with painful periods or PMT, and most difficulties seem to settle down as girls grow older. Many girls in their early teens have irregular periods, and these usually even out given time. There's a great diversity in the age individual girls begin their periods, from as early as nine or ten up until sixteen or seventeen. A lot depends on body weight, and family history plays a part too. Most variations are likely to be perfectly normal, but if you're worried, talk to a professional medical person, if only to set your mind at rest.

Perspective

Events and circumstances, especially distressing ones, can make you feel that the bottom has dropped out of your world. Disappointments, failures, let-downs, break-ups; these can completely floor you and make you feel that nothing will ever be the same again.

Wait a bit before you completely despair. They say time is a great healer and it's true. Pains ease, things do become more bearable. You won't forget the traumas, but you can learn from them and you can become stronger as a result. You may understand why things happened as they did. You may even be allowed to see God's hand at work in the situation. Things look very different when viewed in perspective.

Phone

Adults (and especially parents) just don't seem to appreciate the importance of the phone. They just can't see how essential it is that you contact your friend the moment you get in from school, to continue that fascinating conversation you were having on the bus. They don't think it's neccessary to share each new bit of news with three or four friends, or to get their views on the latest CD, or TV hunk, or hairstyle, or bit of juicy gossip. They don't even sympathise when you're actually doing homework on the phone together! And

they have no patience at all over conversations with boyfriends, especially if your side is mainly made up of remarks like 'Hmm . . .,' 'Well . . .,' 'Perhaps,' 'Did you?' 'You didn't!' Maybe . . .' which drive them into a frenzy wondering what's being said at the other end, and causes them to mutter seriously about installing a payphone!

Prayer

In prayer, we have one of the greatest resources available to the Christian. We can reach God in prayer at anytime, in any place, whatever our need, situation, circumstances or state of mind. In Old Testament times, prayer had to be made through a priest at special times, but since Jesus came we have direct access to God, always.

God loves us to speak to him in prayer. Nothing we can say to him will shock him, upset him, anger him or cause him to love us less. Nothing we can ask is too hard for him to fulfil. If we are bewildered and confused, he understands. If we're angry, he doesn't mind us shouting at him. If we're desperate, he wants to hear from us so that he can begin to do something about it. He wants to hear about it when things are going well too, and share in our delights. We are his children, he's interested in the tiniest details of our lives, and he wants to be involved. (Read 1 Timothy 2:8)

Pregnancy

Pregnancy, sadly, is an all too real fact of life for many girls in their teens. You probably know of girls your age or not much older, who have become pregnant. Pregnancy may be physically possible from the age of puberty, but a young girl is far from ready for the changes and responsibilities that the prospect of becoming a parent brings. A girl is still growing and developing, physically, mentally and emotionally, until her late teens, and needs to be able to complete her own growing before being fully able to sustain another life. Babies need two parents, and young teenage girls are unlikely to have a partner who is mature enough to share in the responsibility of providing and caring for a child. A new life is a gift from God and needs to be well planned and prepared for.

Privacy
See also **Bedrooms**

A bit of privacy does not seem much to ask, but as far as your family's concerned it seems like asking for gold. Your younger siblings consider it their right to burst into your room at any time and help themselves to your belongings, borrow your CD's, and rifle through your cupboards. Even your mum, you suspect, has a quick sift through your personal effects when she comes in to collect the laundry or empty the wastepaper bin. Your sister would certainly read your most private diary if she could ever get her hands on it, ditto your address and phone book. As it is, you have to hide them in a different place every few days, or carry them with you at all times. If you ask for a lock on your door, your dad gets suspicious (what does he think you *do* in there, for goodness' sake?) and your mum worries about fire hazards. All in all, it's easier to go to the public library if you want a bit of peace and quiet. Either that, or lock yourself in the garden shed with a Walkman over your ears!

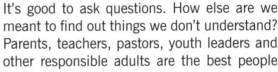

qQ

Quarrels

See **Rows**

Questions

It's good to ask questions. How else are we meant to find out things we don't understand? Parents, teachers, pastors, youth leaders and other responsible adults are the best people to ask, and are usually delighted to answer questions. Maybe it's not too clever to consult others our own age – or at any rate don't lay any bets on getting correct answers! They may be just as much in the dark themselves, though they might not admit it.

God doesn't mind us questioning him either, even if we have our doubts and reservations about him. Reading the New Testament Gospels accounts of the life of Jesus can answer a lot of our questions about the reality and nature of God. (Grab a Bible and have a look through either Matthew, Mark, Luke or John.)

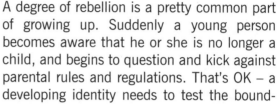

Rebelling

A degree of rebellion is a pretty common part of growing up. Suddenly a young person becomes aware that he or she is no longer a child, and begins to question and kick against parental rules and regulations. That's OK – a developing identity needs to test the boundaries, to see what happens when they decide not to conform, and to experience the result of taking control of their own lives. A certain amount of rebellion is inevitable, and even a healthy sign of normal development.

But it can all get easily out of hand. It's often confusing for both child and parents, and sometimes downright painful. Happily, most teenage rebellion is short-lived and the dust settles again, maybe in a new pattern, but hopefully one that is acceptable to all parties.

Prolonged rebellion, as in the story of the Prodigal Son, is a heartbreaking business and often a sign of stored-up resentment. God's heart aches when his beloved children rebel against him, but, like the father in the parable, he waits eagerly with open arms for the rebellious one to return. (Read Luke 15:11-24.)

Relationships

See also
Boyfriends

Relationships (meaning the boy/girl variety) are a main pre-occupation with all young people and often cause a lot of aggro. Everyone needs someone to be close to and to share with. Parents do not always realise the seriousness of teenage relationships, or the depth of pain involved when one comes to an end. You may be young, but things can hurt just as much as when they happen to older people. Remarks like 'There are plenty more fish in the sea' seldom help much, especially when the only fish you're remotely interested in has swum away leaving you high and dry.

A friend with a sympathetic ear and shoulder is usually the biggest comfort when things aren't going so well. And time, and prayer, and not being in too much of a hurry to look for another relationship.

Religions

See also **Cults**

You will rub shoulders with many people of other religions in today's multi-cultural society. The increasing practice in most schools is to include all religions in their acts of worship. The religious faiths of other people are to be respected. It serves no purpose to zealously denounce any belief that is not our own, or to constantly criticise and point out its failings.

On the other hand, we need to remember that the only way to God is through acceptance of Jesus Christ as our personal saviour. A hotch-potch of doctrines picked from other religions, however attractive, will not do.

Christ is the living Saviour who changes lives, not just a religion of rules and rituals and ideals. By his Holy Spirit, we can live lives that stand out, so that others notice, and hopefully, want to know more.

Reputation

See *also*
Peer Pressure

Once lost, a reputation cannot usually be regained very easily. There are people who watch your every move and need no encouragement to blacken your name. Best not to provide fuel, even a little bit. Respect yourself and stay away from anything you know to be wrong and harmful. Mud sticks.

However, memories are short and others will probably forget before you do. If you've done wrong, ask God's forgiveness, forgive yourself, and ask God to help you forgive others.

Rows

Most people fall out with someone else from time to time. Most often, it'll be someone we're close to; a family member or a friend. It wouldn't be human nature if everyone agreed with everyone else about everything, all the time.

Just the same, rows and quarrels can be upsetting, especially if they go on and on, and involve other people taking sides. It's childish and silly to sulk and refuse to speak to someone you've fallen out with. OK, so you're hurting, and you feel it was the other person's fault and therefore their place to say sorry first; they probably feel exactly the same. No one wants to be the first to apologise, and the rift gets wider. It's cool to have the guts to make the first move and you'll probably be pleasantly surprised at the results.

Rules

Rules are made to be broken, or so the saying goes. Rules are also laid down for a purpose, usually the protection and well-being of those asked to abide by them. Sticking to the rules will not necessarily cramp your style. In fact you may find that in doing so you will gain trust and, in the long run, more freedom.

sS

School

See also **Teachers**

A person spends on average, twelve to fourteen years at school, not counting college or university. That's a good slice out of your life.

You may love school or hate it. It may seem the ultimate in restriction or the greatest opportunity and challenge. You may be in a well-ordered private school or a concrete jungle, or anywhere in between.

It really does pay off to work at school. Although missed opportunities can always be taken up later, our school years are the time when our brain and intellect are best able to absorb and retain information, and the time when we're free of other responsibilities, such as earning a living or maintaining a home and family. We have the freedom to follow our dreams and the means to work towards realising them. Schools have technology and resources freely available for our use, and support and encouragement to pursue the studies of our choice. School provides lasting friendships and can offer support when things may be difficult at home or elsewhere. Sadly, we maybe value our schooldays most when we have moved on to the more challenging environments of college or university, or out into the big wide world.

Self-esteem

There are some strange ideas around about self-esteem, even in Christian circles. We may have been told not to be big-headed or to have too high an opinion of ourselves, or have had it impressed upon us that we should always put others first. (A tall order!) We're not meant to be inordinately full of ourselves, but being unnaturally humble isn't what self-esteem is all about either. We're probably only too aware of our faults and failings, without the put-downs that life often throws at us. Maybe what we need is to see ourselves as God sees us.

Each one of us is precious to God and he loves us just the way we are. It's been said though, that he loves us too much to leave us the way we are. As soon as we decide to follow Jesus, he's in the business of transforming us into the kind of people he intended us to be in the first place.

God wants us to remember how much he cares for us, and to respect ourselves accordingly. We may be born sinners, but we are now covered with the righteousness of Jesus. We're OK people in God's eyes and we need to be able to reckon ourselves valuable in order to be able to reckon others. (Read Matthew 10:29-31.)

Sex

God created us male and female, and approved of the differences. His view was that he'd done a very good thing. He'd given us sex as a wonderful gift, to be used and shared and enjoyed within the security and commitment of lifelong marriage.

This gift of sex has been cheapened and

77

exploited and altered from God's original plan. The sex drive is a powerful human force and is seen everywhere in today's society – not just in films, but adverts and magazines too. Sex sells. This cheapening of sex has ruined lives and shattered relationships, a tragic result of ignoring God's laws concerning the use of sex.

As Christians, we need to stand firm and not to be drawn into the values and moral standards of this fallen world. It's easy to go with the crowd, but even more worthwhile waiting to share sex only with that special person who is to be your chosen life partner. (Read Matthew 5:27-37, John 8:1-11 and 2 Samuel 11:1-15.)

Shopping

Most of us find that there is nothing like a bit of 'retail therapy' for cheering up a fit of the blues. A new top or pair of jeans can put a spring back in the step and a sparkle in the eye, even if they're only from a market or charity shop.

It makes a difference who you go shopping with, of course. Shopping with your mum is usually a definite no-no, and other relatives for company aren't too cool either. Neither is a boyfriend the best person to shop with – just notice how many fellas there are always hanging out round the doorways of the High Street boutiques, blocking the way and looking bored!

The best shopping companion is perhaps your best friend, especially if she's honest enough to tell you that the little top you fancy so much tends to turn your complexion to the colour of mud, makes your upper arms look gigantic and will probably lose its wonderful velvety pile in the very first wash! After all, what are friends for?!

Sin
See also **Evil**

We don't like to talk about sin, do we? It's not at all comfortable to face up to the fact that we're all sinners, but we only have to look at the world around us to know it's true. The human race has messed up, and it's all down to sin in the human heart.

There's a remedy, though. God sent his son into the world to live a sinless human life and so be able to become a perfect sacrifice for all our sin. Because of him we can go free, our sins forgiven and forgotten. With Jesus in our lives, we can make a real difference to a sick and sinful world.

Sisters

Your sister may be your best friend or your worst enemy. Your feelings may also be quite ambiguous – maybe you're the best of mates one minute and at each other's throats the next. It is not always easy being a sister, especially if you have to share a room. Often that spills over into sharing other things like clothes, make-up, books, hairdryers, CDs – sometimes voluntarily but too often without permission from the other, resulting in more rows. Your sister usually knows you very well. It may be possible to pull the wool over your parents' eyes but not your sister's.

On the other hand, when life is getting you down and all other comfort fails, your sister will probably be the one who's there for you with a comforting shoulder and a big box of tissues.

Smoking

Smoking is an addictive habit and it's also an anti-social one. Sadly, it is more widespread among teenage girls than boys. Smoking is closely linked with lung cancer, from which there are 100,000 deaths per year. Some of these will not even themselves be smokers, but will have suffered the results of inhaling other people's cigarette smoke.

Smoke also clings to clothes, hair and furnishings and changes breath and body odour. Giving up smoking may not always be easy, but it can be done, and will pay dividends.

Soaps

Soaps are required viewing for most girls, and can provide a relaxing hour after a busy day, especially as most seem to happen in Australia, with settings of sun-baked beaches, white surf, and a succession of gorgeous bronzed fellas!

Maybe a good idea is not to take them too seriously, though. It's easy to feel that our relationships can be sorted, broken hearts mended, dangers overcome and happiness restored, with all loose ends tied up neatly, because that's what happens on TV. It's largely fantasy, though the situations may be realistically portrayed. Soap operas may be fun to watch and good entertainment, but real life they ain't.

Spots

See **Acne**

Stress

See also **Panic, Fear, Depression**

Most of us feel stressed out at some time or other. Stress can have many causes, from family problems and relationship difficulties to exam pressure or bereavement. Even happy occasions like parties or holidays can cause a degree of stress. Some stress is inevitable, but too much can cause real problems. If things are getting on top of you and causing a high level of stress, you may feel tired, run down, tearful, moody, depressed or unusually agressive. You may feel tension in the muscles of your neck, shoulders and back and you may have difficulty sleeping. Some people believe that alcohol, smoking, or drugs can help relax someone who is tense, but this is an illusion. These substances may help short-term, but will cause more stress and damage our bodies in the long run.

Get advice from your doctor. Talk to a teacher or tutor if work is bothering you. Try some outdoor activity or a work-out at a gym. Don't be too shy to ask for prayer from your church or Christian youth group.

Suffering

One of the most common questions asked of Christians is why God allows suffering, especially when it happens to innocent people, i.e. children, or famine victims, or war casualties, or the elderly?

It's a hard one to answer and often we can't. We know though, that God's heart breaks over the suffering that he sees in his children. He gave us the gift of free will and the responsibility of choice. All of us can either accept God into our lives or reject him. Sadly, the majority still refuse to accept him. We may get angry with God over the suffering we see in the world, but if we're honest, isn't it often the result of man's greed, hatred, and the turning away from God's laws?
(Read 1 Peter 3:8-22.)

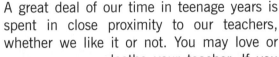

tT

Teachers
See also **School**

A great deal of our time in teenage years is spent in close proximity to our teachers, whether we like it or not. You may love or loathe your teacher. If you are fortunate enough to have a real rapport with your teacher, he or she can be a real inspiration and help in achieving your chosen goals. There may be a few sadistic bullies among teachers, though maybe not as many as you would like to think. A teacher can be a good confidante, example and encourager as well as actually instructing you. Remember though, that they're not supermen and women! They're only human and may have bad days too.

Thank You

Thank you is not too difficult to say, but is something often overlooked. These two words can make a lot of difference. Saying thanks for a present or card, help or advice, friendly support, or even thanking a parent or teacher who's been there for you, not only encourages the giver but makes you feel good too. Most of all, God deserves our thanks for his unconditional love. (Read Luke 17:11-19.)

Travel
See also **Holidays**

They say that travel broadens the mind. It also lightens the pocket and causes many a grey hair and wrinkle to the parents, especially if the traveller has set off with only a backpack, high hopes, and no forwarding address.

Some people are born travellers and some like to stay put. The fortunate ones get to go on holidays abroad, usually a vast improvement on family holidays in general. School exchanges are an excellent means of sampling another way of life, a different (preferably warmer) climate, unusual food, learning another language and gaining confidence along the way. You'll be free of parental interference too, though if you're with a family, your host parents will take on that responsibility.

There are other ways of seeing the world, too; notably the summer projects and missions organised by various Christian organisations, when a group or team of young people participate in helping Third World or European countries in a variety of 'hands on' ways. You will probably have to be very fit, a committed Christian, and will have to be prepared to work hard and raise your own funds for the trip, but this kind of adventure can be most fulfilling, enriching and rewarding, and will probably alter your perspective on life for good.

uU

UFOs

Stories abound about Unidentified Flying Objects, and all kinds of other extra-terrestrial phenomena, fuelled by a flood of books, videos and movies. We do not know if there is life beyond our galaxy, though wonders of new discovery daily unfold before our eyes through science, technology and space travel. The Bible speaks of the planets and stars, but it does not say whether or not life exists on them. Whether or not, it is all under the control and Lordship of our creator God.

Ugly

Beauty is supposed to be in the eye of the beholder, and maybe ugliness is too. Most teenage girls, however much of a babe they may seem to others, are prone to peering into mirrors and uttering cries of despair over their appearance.

A spot or two, or a misjudged hair colour, even the inherited shape of a nose, can convince you you're the most unattractive object ever!

Don't you believe it! You are lovely in God's sight, and very probably lovely in the sight of others too.

University   If you're the academic type, the prospect of university will loom, maybe even before you've sat your GCSEs. The variety of locations, courses and combinations of courses is enormous. Get hold of some prospectuses. Studying them is quite an education in itself.

vV

Valentines

Hearts beat faster as Valentine's Day comes round again. How many pink or red or blue, heart-shaped or frilly, funny or romantic (or even rude) cards will plop through your letterbox this year? Will you know who they're from, or will you be left guessing and tantalised? What happens (horrors!) if no one sends you a Valentine? Or what if you find out that that one you've been puzzling over turns out to be only from your mum?

Then there's the problem of deciding who you're going to send one (or more than one) to, the choice of card, the wording of the cryptic message to put inside, and the delicious anticipation of wondering whether the recipient will guess it's from you. Better give him a clue, just in case.

Vegetarianism

See also **Diets, Food, Cooking**

Many people opt for vegetarianism today, especially young people. Vegetarians do not eat red meat in any form, though some may eat a little chicken or fish. Vegans have much stricter rules, omitting even fish, eggs and dairy products.

You may choose to be vegetarian for reasons of conscience, i.e. as a protest against meat raised in an intensive factory-type environment. You may think a meat-free diet

Vegetarianism

is healthier, or you may simply dislike meat. The Bible rules allow for meat eating but don't insist upon it. It's a personal choice.

If you've decided on vegetarianism, make sure you have alternative proteins and vitamins in your diet. Cheese, cereals, pasta, pulses, soya products, fruits and vegetables, will provide what is necessary for proper nutrition and good health.

Verbal Abuse
See also **Bullying**

No one, but no one should feel they have to put up with verbal abuse. It can be one of the most hurtful of things, and is a very unpleasant aspect of bullying. People who are different in some way that makes them stand out from the crowd are often targets for verbal abuse. It's cowardly and it's cheap.

Christians often come in for their share, or more than their share. If possible, draw strength from other Christians. We're told to pray for those who treat us badly. If you're vulnerable and you're really getting upset by verbal abuse, something should be done. Tell a teacher, a tutor or a parent. This kind of nastiness should be firmly nipped in the bud.

Videos

There's nothing more relaxing than curling up with a good video to watch and maybe a box of chocs. In your parents' day, the only films you could watch were what happened to be showing at the cinema or on TV – which had only two or three channels!

Now there's a whole array to choose from at your video-hire shop. Choose well, and don't be tempted to try the dubious stuff. It's easy to get hooked on nasties without perhaps meaning to. What you look at helps to make you what you are. Happy viewing!

Voice

It's a shock to hear your voice on tape for the first time. Can those squeaky, giggly, alien-sounding tones really be the way you speak? Is that what your boyfriend hears every time he talks to you on the telephone?

Don't be too quick to rush out and book elocution lessons. There's nothing wrong with your voice and there's nothing wrong with a regional accent. Be proud of your background. Don't try to talk posh. It'll sound dafter than ever and you'll only get stressed out trying to keep it up.

wW

War

There have always been wars, and always will be. In the pages of Scripture and down through history, war has followed war. There are resources enough for everyone on our earth, but something in the heart of humankind pushes us to fight our fellows time and again.

Most people don't want war but are powerless in the face of the activated war machine. We may launch protests and campaign for peace, but change will only come when the hearts of individuals are transformed by knowing the Lord Jesus Christ. Only in his kingdom will war cease.

Weddings
See also **Marriage**

Most girls dream of their wedding, and most have a picture of floating down the aisle in a romantic cloud of white tulle and satin, the beginnings of living happily ever after.

In reality, most weddings are rather more stressful than this. There are likely to be hitches. The best man may lose his way en route to the church, or the small page boy may terrorise the little bridesmaids. Elderly Uncle Henry may fall asleep and snore during the ceremony and the mothers will certainly shed embarrassing tears.

Despite everything, wedding days are usually looked back on as one of the happiest days of

Weddings

a girl's life. However the wedding ceremony went, the important point is that a marriage has been entered into, which will hopefully be a mutual joy, comfort and support to both husband and wife for the rest of their lives.

Why?

See **Questions**

Work

See also **Careers**

Unless you're the least motivated person on earth, everyone enjoys work of some kind or other. It may be physical, pottering in the kitchen or taking a car engine to pieces. Or it may be mental work, doing crosswords or writing a best-seller. School and college work looms large all through your teen years, and you will probably have work experience or Saturday and holiday jobs to earn some cash for yourself. Sooner or later, you'll be projected into the big world where everyone works for real to keep a roof over their head and food on the table. Now is the time to prepare for that, aiming for the best qualifications so that you ultimately find and enjoy the work you're best suited for.

Worries
See also
Fear, Panic

Worship

Worship is an essential part of knowing God, who created us just for that purpose. When we have a relationship with Jesus Christ, it is natural to want to worship him for what he has done and above all, for what he is. We can worship God in many ways; in prayer, singing, clapping, dancing, with instruments or creative gifts, with others or quietly on our own.

Worship focuses upon God and brings a sense of his presence in a way that perhaps nothing else can. Worship is an important part of their experience for most Christian young people. They are usually less inhibited than older people and less bound by tradition. Worshipping God, alone or with others, is one of the most precious and meaningful privileges afforded to us. (Read Psalm 47)

Wrinklies

They're old (and they act like it), well past it, out of touch, dated and inhibited. They don't like or understand loud music, late nights, enthusiasm, trendy gear, some of your friends or any of your culture.

They're also experienced, long-suffering, not as daft as you may think, hard-working and caring. They know a thing or two. (Well, they brought you up, didn't they?)

X – The Unknown Quantity

See also **Occult**

There's a great deal of interest these days in the supernatural and the unexplained. It's probably because we've all grown weary of the materialistic, and are looking for a spiritual dimension in this post-modern age.

Don't be fooled! The only genuine supernatural experience is the one we enter into by becoming reconciled to God through his son.

yY

Youth Groups

A good Christian Youth Group is perhaps the best asset a young believer can have. The group will supply strength, fellowship, encouragement and support. A wise leader will gain the confidence of the individual members, give an ear to listen, and advice and prayer if needed. A group provides much-needed discussion, friendship and fun. You'll go on holidays and outings, to conferences and houseparties together. If one falters, there'll be others who are strong.

If you're not fortunate enough to have a group nearby, find another Christian so that you can support one another as prayer partners. It could even be someone you keep in touch with by letter.

zZ

Zits
See **Acne**

Some contact addresses and phone numbers

Aids

National AIDS helpline: (0800) 567123.

The Red Admiral Project: 51a Philibeach Gardens, London SW5 9ED. (0171-835) 1495 Provides free specialist counselling for anyone affected by HIV/AIDS.

Alcohol Abuse

Alcoholics Anonymous (AA), London Helpline: (0171-352) 3001. Head Office, PO Box 1, Stonebow House, York YO1 7NJ. (01904) 644026.

Alcohol Action Wales, 8th Floor, Brunel House, 2 Fitzlan Rd, Cardiff CF2 1EB.

Childline

Childline: (0800) 1111. Freepost 1111, London N1 ORR.

NSPCC Childline: (0800) 800500.

Drug Abuse

Lifeline: (0161-839) 2054.

Re-Solv (Society for prevention of solvent and volatile substance abuse): 30a High St, Stone, Staffs ST15 8AW.

Eating Disorders	Youth helpline: (01603) 765050. Mon-Fri, 4-6 pm.
	The Eating Disorder Association: First Floor, Wensum House, 103 Prince of Wales Rd, Norwich, Norfolk NR1 1DW. (01603) 621414
	The Anorexia and Bulimia Nervosa Association, Tottenham Women and Health Centre Annexe, Tottenham, London N15 4RK.
Pregnancy Advice	British Pregnancy Advisory Service: (0345) 304030.
Giving up Smoking	Smoker's Quitline: Wales, (01222) 641888. London, (0171-487) 3000.
	ASH (Action for Smoking and Health): 5-11 Mortimer St, London W1A 4QW.
Christian Holidays and Mission Projects	Scripture Union: 207-209 Queensway, Bletchley, Milton Keynes MK2 2EB. Tel: (01908) 856000. Fax: (01908) 856111.
	Crusaders (Cruesoe): 2 Romeland Hill, St. Albans, Herts AL3 4ET.
	World Horizons, North Dock Centre, Llanelli, Dyfed.
	Eleanor Watkins can be contacted through the publisher's address at the front of the book.